Alfred Thomas Tucker Wise

Davos Platz

And the effects of high altitude on phthisis

Alfred Thomas Tucker Wise

Davos Platz
And the effects of high altitude on phthisis

ISBN/EAN: 9783742892119

Manufactured in Europe, USA, Canada, Australia, Japa

Cover: Foto ©ninafisch / pixelio.de

Manufactured and distributed by brebook publishing software (www.brebook.com)

Alfred Thomas Tucker Wise

Davos Platz

AND THE

EFFECTS OF HIGH ALTITUDE

ON

PHTHISIS

BY

ALFRED WISE, M.D.,

LICENTIATE OF THE ROYAL COLLEGE OF PHYSICIANS LONDON; MEMBER OF THE
ROYAL COLLEGE OF SURGEONS OF ENGLAND; VISITING PHYSICIAN TO
THE INFIRMARY FOR CONSUMPTION, MARGARET ST., CAVENDISH SQUARE;
LATE PHYSICIAN TO THE WESTERN GENERAL DISPENSARY;
LATE HONORARY MEDICAL OFFICER TO THE KILBURN AND MAIDA VALE
DISPENSARY; LATE HOUSE PHYSICIAN, HOUSE SURGEON, AND RESIDENT
OBSTETRIC OFFICER, ST. MARY'S HOSPITAL, LONDON; MEMBER OF
THE HARVEIAN SOCIETY, ETC., ETC.

LONDON
J. & A. CHURCHILL
NEW BURLINGTON STREET

PREFACE

At the commencement of the winter of 1879 tho author visited Davos, for the purpose of making observations of the climate, &c.

From the notes then made and during a residence there in the winter of 1880, the following pages are compiled, with the hope that they may contain some information which may not altogether prove uninteresting to those who view the treatment of phthisis at high altitudes with favour.

 82, Sutherland Gardens,
  London, W.;
   July, 1881.

CONTENTS

CHAPTER I
SITE AND ELEVATION OF DAVOS—WATER, DRAINAGE, AND ACCOMMODATION 1

CHAPTER II
ATMOSPHERE, SUNLIGHT, WIND, ETC. . . . 6

CHAPTER III
A CURSORY GLANCE AT PHTHISIS . . 13

CHAPTER IV
THERAPEUTIC EFFECTS OF COLD . . 16

CHAPTER V
SUNLIGHT 24

CHAPTER VI
BAROMETRIC PRESSURE—OXYGEN AND OZONE . 27

CHAPTER VII
METEOROLOGICAL CONDITIONS AT HIGH ALTITUDES, AND THEIR EFFECTS ON THE LUNGS—THE THERMOMETER AND THE SENSATION OF COLD . 38

CHAPTER VIII
THE "DRAWBACKS" OF DAVOS . . . 47

WEATHER REPORTS FOR 1880 . . . 55

DAVOS PLATZ

CHAPTER I

SITE AND ELEVATION OF DAVOS PLATZ, WATER, DRAINAGE, AND ACCOMMODATION

THE district of Davos (an elevated valley in the Grisons in Switzerland) extends to about fourteen miles in length, and contains between 3000 and 4000 inhabitants. The three miles of valley, with the health resort, Davos am Platz, has an altitude of 5100 feet, and is surrounded by alps ranging to nearly 9000 feet above sea-level.

This portion of the valley is effectually sheltered from the north and west winds, rather less so from the south and east.

Numerous "Châlets" are scattered about on all sides. The village—Davos—is situated on the north-western side of the valley, and consists chiefly of hotels and "pensions;" of these there are four or five large hotels aud several other "pensions" affording fair accommodation.

The place is frequented principally by Germans and Swiss; and the hotels, filled entirely by English, are three in number.

The scenery is picturesque and grand, although somewhat limited in extent, the valley in this part varying from 500 to 1000 yards broad.

Thousands of pine trees cover the steep slopes, and a winding stream, the "Landwasser," drains a lake at the north-east end of the valley.

The soil is dry and thin, excepting the central portion, where it is of a peaty character.

Nearly the whole extent is utilised for cattle grazing aud hay, and is well drained from surface moisture.

The water-supply of the houses is upland surface-water, falling mostly as snow; the loss of air by freezing is compensated by aëration in its precipitous course from the mountains.

These streams are constant, both in summer and winter, and should furnish this necessity in as pure a state as could be desired; one would judge it to be so from its taste and appearance.

Davos may consider itself fortunate in possessing a water naturally pure and unlikely to be tainted, except in the storage.

The streams are situated in deep hollows on the Alps, and from their inaccessible positions are unlikely to be contamiuated by cattle. In the winter no cattle are anywhere in the vicinity of these rills, and the storage at this season of the year may be considered comparatively safe, as the water remains but a short time in the house tanks, taps being constantly allowed to flow to avert the inevitable consequence of pipes freezing if their contents were allowed to be at a standstill.

For a scant population the present system of drainage, although a most inefficient mode of removing excreta, may not be considered dangerous under the existing circumstances. Cesspools are mostly used, and the deposit utilised for manure in the spring of the year, and occasionally during the autumn months. The absorbent nature of the soil, the low temperature, and fresh air, soon deodorise this manure and render it innocuous; but if such proccedings were practised in a temperate or warm climate, among a thickly populated community, serious results would be experienced.

The dry earth system is adopted at one or two hotels, and this plan, if carried out with care, is unattended with danger.

A small population in a healthy locality, with the oxidising results of the air, the absorbent nature of the soil, and antiseptic powers of a low temperature, may certainly trifle to an alarming extent in sanitary matters.

Hotel accommodation at Davos has greatly improved of late years. From a gradual increase of the number of English who resort there for the season, English tastes and habits have been more studied by the hotel proprietors than formerly. Food is good and plentiful, whey and good milk may be obtained in sufficient quantities, and the wines are various both in quality and price.

CHAPTER II

ATMOSPHERE, SUNLIGHT, AND WIND

As the purity, freshness, and stimulating properties of the atmosphere are important points for consideration, attention must be directed to its particular characters of humidity, temperature, barometric pressure, sunlight, wind, &c.

On the rate of movement and moisture of air much depends as to the temperature which is agreeable to the sensations. Rapidly moving air abstracts heat in proportion to its velocity. A cold atmosphere which is damp creates the impression of a much lower temperature than it really is. High winds, with damp or cold air, give rise to chills (with their train of evils) and feelings of discomfort.

The quantity of moisture in the air, affecting, as it does, the rate of evaporation from the lungs and skin, is a point which requires much consideration; but at present observations have been so limited that we have not much data to go upon.

Certainly, warm moist air is sometimes very grateful to cases of congestion or irritability of the bronchial tubes; but a more permanent condition of moisture, of which our English winter affords an example, undoubtedly has an injurious influence on the majority of lung diseases, the watery vapour abstracting an undue amount of heat from the respiratory tract and giving rise to catarrhs, coughs, or perhaps inflammations.

It is a generally accepted fact that dampness of soil, apart from hereditary tendency, favours the development of phthisis.

This dampness supplying the atmosphere with large quantities of moisture, shows what an important observation in climatic influences "humidity" becomes in its results on the mitigation or development of that disease. Now, it may be expected that in a place where the surface formation is favorable for the rapid escape of surface-water, where dry snow covers the ground, and the rainfall is slight, the reverse of this condition, so pernicious to the lungs, might be expected.

In the high altitudes of Switzerland, although an occasional thaw or fall of snow may saturate the air with moisture, proof of the general dryness is seen from the low percentage of "relative humidity," illustrating both the absence of damp winds and a minimum of watery vapour evaporated from underfoot.

What the precise pathological effects are of the incessant breathing of moist air is not yet quite clear; but it has been shown that bacteria and germs flourish in such a medium, whilst cold and dryness are antagonistic to their development or increase.

Excessive cooling of a part of the respiratory tract from moisture, on account of the conduction of heat being more free in a damp atmosphere, is frequently experienced when breathing a cold London fog, the sensation of cold being felt sometimes as far down as the notch of the sternum and even lower.

The result on the skin is to abstract an undue amount of heat and retard the normal evaporation of waste products, thereby throwing more work on the lungs and kidneys.

Although there is a diminished death rate from phthisis in some parts of Scotland and Ireland, where excessive dampness prevails, we shall, on inquiry, find that in these districts the people are employed mostly in out-door pursuits; but if a phthisical patient courted extreme ventilation in a damp climate the result would not be so satisfactory as exposure to drier surroundings. Perhaps it is hardly necessary to mention that air containing less than 35 per cent. of moisture, with the temperature at 60°, is much too dry for health and would give rise to irritation of the air-passages.

The freedom or otherwise of air, from germs, mechanical irritants, noxious gases or animal exhalations, necessitates but little discussion, the presence of these contaminations rendering the air impure in proportion to their quantity.

One cannot help observing that the dust of London and other large towns, composed, as it mostly is, of pulverised granite and horse-droppings, people inhale without much complaint, but no doubt as hygienic laws become better appreciated, attention may be directed to this offensive and injurious pollution of town air.

Intimately connected with the subject of pure air is that of ventilation.

Receiving, as it does in England, some scientific attention, many persons would be led to expect that a perfect system existed in any place laying claim to a health-resort. Now this is by no means the case in Switzerland. Like elsewhere, much depends on the individual as to the amount of air which he considers advantageous or the reverse. In his private rooms he may exercise this discretion at will; but in dining or sitting rooms, and especially smoking and billiard rooms, any thirsty display by an individual for fresh air is usually objected to by some one present. This occurs both at home and abroad.

Deserving, as the subject is, of the greatest consideration, it is to be regretted that so little real attention is paid to it.

The purity of air in the interior of buildings both in health and disease, and especially in the treatment of chest affections, demands every scrutiny when we take into account the number of hours spent in-doors.

The hotels at Davos, however, are not over-crowded nor badly ventilated; although an improvement in the latter direction would be desirable, but much time is spent out of the house.

On many of the cold days with the thermometer standing at 20° or 25° Fahr. in the shade, and a still atmosphere, the sun radiation is very powerful and enables many persons to sit in the open air without great coats or wraps, the only precaution necessary being the use of a pair of dark spectacles to neutralise the glare of the snow.

Great benefit is derived on these occasions from the fresh air and sunlight, air which may be considered comparatively free from the usual contaminations.

The great depth of snow buries all impurities, the noxious gases of which are destroyed or lie dormant until the spring thaw. Frequent falls of snow during the winter keep all surface refuse, as it were, below ground. The cold renders inert organic germs in the atmosphere, which have escaped the process of filtration by the fall of snow. There is a freedom from dust, with the exception of a trifling quantity of carbon specs from the chimneys.

These conditions are healthy and exhilarating, and the mental effect of the sunlight on many patients who have been habitually spending much of their time in-doors at home, is most cheering and beneficial.

The value of exposure to fresh air in many diseases is becoming more widely known and appreciated, and its benefit to phthisical cases, provided they escape attacks of catarrh and bronchitis, &c., cannot be doubted.

CHAPTER III

CURSORY VIEW OF PHTHISIS

A FEW words on phthisis may not be out of place before speaking of barometric pressure, sunlight, and cold air.

In the term phthisis here is included the variety of morbid conditions which came under this designation, with the exception of the acute forms.

A great deal has been done of late years in the treatment of this disease, but some of us in the present day may be inclined to view the complaint with little interest, following the usual routine treatment, with, in many cases, a reasonable misgiving as to the permanent result likely to ensue.

This is not to be wondered at when we take into consideration the state of nutrition generally accompanying the malady.

Indeed, the modern German school so far

mistrusts the efficacy of drugs in phthisis, that it is only for urgent symptoms their use is recommended, reliance being placed in change of air and exercise—mountain air, if possible—accompanied by cold douche baths, and gentle gymnastics.

It would appear that the following group of symptoms in chronic phthisis have an intimate association with high altitude treatment. They are—

Mal-assimilation of food
Loss of appetite;
Night sweats and pyrexia;
Loss of flesh;
Dyspepsia and debility; and
Imperfect sanguification.

That these symptoms have a powerful bearing on the future course of the disease and its treatment seems clear; most of them are expressed by the general term "malnutrition," and the diet and remedies from which we might expect marked results are not assimilated in the alimentary tract, sometimes even passing through the intestines unchanged, or producing symptoms requiring their discontinuance.

In such cases as these the local lesion has the upper hand for a time, for until the nutrition begins to mend we cannot hope for much progress towards recovery of the damaged lung, for it would appear that amelioration of the latter is frequently preceded by improvement in nutrition; although where there is an absorption of inflammatory products in the lungs, pyrexia and wasting, with loss of appetite, &c., may continue for a period depending entirely on the quantity of poisonous material circulating in the blood.

A push to nutrition may be observed when nourishing diet, milk, cod-liver oil, &c., are so serviceable, and when pancreatine or pancreatic emulsion (assisting the absorption of fats which are so essential to the frame) give the first evidences of progression by the patient gaining in weight, assuring us then a certain amount of hopefulness in the case.

CHAPTER IV

THERAPEUTICAL EFFECTS OF COLD

IN returning to the subject of climate, attention must be directed to the effects of moderate cold on nutrition, pyrexia and perspiration.

Cold increases the appetite, probably from its exhilarating powers and the requirements in the body of more hydrocarbons to meet a normal increase in combustion.

A well-known writer on therapeutics remarks that the most vigorous health is maintained by a rapid construction and destruction of tissue within certain bounds, provided these processes are fairly balanced. Cold, when judiciously applied, is well known to be a powerful tonic. A cold climate and cold bathing are tonic and bracing.

The theory of the tonic action of cold may, perhaps, be stated thus:—During exposure to cold the loss of body-heat, as tested by the thermometer, is by no means a measure of the quantity withdrawn.

Many observers have shown that at such times increased combustion occurs, whereby much of the lost heat is compensated, and the temperature is maintained as soon as restored. This increased oxidation of tissue is demonstrated by the greatly increased quantity of carbonic acid thrown off by the lungs on exposure to cold (Ringer).

Cold may also be included under the heading of nervine tonics, as it stimulates the nervous system, abolishing that languor and want of energy that heat produces, the most striking example being the "plunge" or "cold douche" after a Turkish bath, and also the capacity for exertion that one possesses in a cold climate.

With regard to the effects on the Anglo-Saxon and Celtic races of going to live in a climate with a lower mean temperature and greater variations than their own, we have the experiences of Canada, Nova Scotia, and some parts of the North American States.

In all these, if food is good and plentiful, health is not only sustained, but perhaps improved. The agricultural and out-door life of Canada or Nova Scotia is probably the cause of this; but certain it is that in those countries the European not only enjoys health, but produces a progeny as vigorous, if not more so, than that of the parent race (Parkes).

These statements can be endorsed by many familiar with the experiences of Canada and Nova Scotia. Absence of crowded towns, dry, cold, and pure air, with good food, are circumstances which everywhere contribute to health.

With regard to sanguification, a low temperature causes the lungs to absorb more oxygen, and by thus inducing quicker change in the blood-corpuscles, exerts some influence on anæmia.

By the low percentage of humidity and the absence of strong currents of air in the high valleys of Switzerland the low temperature is by no means disagreeable, and but rarely gives rise to the clammy moist skin of exposed parts, which is so often experienced in England, and is one of the chief causes of the consciousness of a low temperature.

Many who would be unable to withstand a freezing temperature in England without feeling intensely chilled are enabled to take gentle exercise or sit in the open air. As less heat is abstracted from the body by the infrequency of cold winds animal heat is comfortably maintained in the open air by those who would otherwise be incapable of taking sufficient exercise to keep themselves warm.

There is also less liability to temporary congestion of the internal organs (brought about by the chilling effects of currents of cold air).

In a windy climate these frequent surface coolings with transitory contractions of the cutaneous vessels, although insignificant to a person in moderate health, may be of some consequence to lungs perhaps already having a tendency to blood stasis.

In the late Arctic expedition dry, still air, many degrees below zero, could be comfortably borne. The late Dr Moss, who accompanied the expedition, says: "In comfortable winter quarters, and with plenty of dry clothing, we found the extremest cold rather curious and interesting than painful or dangerous. An icy tub on an English winter morning feels colder to the skin than the calm Arctic air. Cold alone never interrupted daily exercise; it was possible to walk for two or three hours over our snow-clad hills, in a temperature of 100° below freezing, without getting a single frostbite or perceptibly lowering the temperature of the body."[1]

It has been noticed that many patients lose their night-sweats and high temperatures in Davos—sometimes after a few days' residence.

It is not unlikely that the lower temperature of the surrounding medium, viz. the atmosphere, amongst other causes, influences this to some extent, and also, in the cases of excessive perspirations, that its stimulating properties brace up the coats of the cutaneous

[1] 'Shores of the Polar Sea,' p. 47.

vessels and promote a healthy action of the skin and sudoriparous glands.

Some analogy appears to exist between the action of cold on temperatures and the effects of quinine and salicylic acid; all these therapeutic agents reduce a high temperature, but have a markedly diminished action on the normal heat of the body.

Fothergill remarks, in his excellent work on therapeutics, that "The whole subject of body heat—its production, its dispersion, and their disturbances—call for more general attention than they have yet succeeded in attracting."

This hint forcibly suggests the careful consideration of the high temperatures in phthisis and the rational means for their reduction.

There is evidence that the interchange of gases between the air and the blood through the skin has an important share in keeping up the temperature of the body, and we find the temperature of the surface much elevated in cases of pneumonia, phthisis, &c.,

in which the lungs seem to perform their function very insufficiently.[1]

It seems probable that, in addition to the cooler surrounding atmosphere playing its part, and causing a general increase of the quantity of blood in the lungs, that the lessened barometric pressure accelerates the action of osmosis in an impaired and imperfect lung, and compensates, to some extent, for its loss in volume, for we know that a more rapid interchange of gases takes place under a reduced pressure.

In the consideration of cold climates for phthisis it is well to remember that some forms of this disease run a rapid course in hot climates.

According to Rattray[2] there is a lessened proportion of blood and a large proportion of air in the lungs in the tropics, and this is borne out by the fact of the lessened weight of the lungs of Europeans in the tropics (Dr Francis, Bengal Army).

[1] Carpenter's 'Human Physiology.'
[2] "On the Effects and Change of Climate on the Human Economy," by A. Rattray, M.D., R.N., 'Proceedings of the Royal Society,' Nos. 122, 126, 139 (1869—1872).

There is, however, no decided criterion for the determination of the question whether—

1. A major quantity of blood in the lungs, such as may be diffused through theso organs in a high cold climate, with slightly augmented freedom (from acceleration of respiratory and cardiac movements) and more complete oxidation, is or is not less disposed to bring about pulmonary hæmorrhage than—

2. A minor proportion of blood at sea-level, circulating with less facility, and not so effectually oxidised.

Tho problem also appears to present itself as ono of "nutrition of tho lung," viz. whether slight hyperæmia (under those circumstances) is not a more desirable sequence than the inclination to slight blood stasis of No. 2.

CHAPTER V

SUNLIGHT

That light has an action on the blood-corpuscles may be easily proved by observing the large number of workers in mines and dark factories, shop girls, clerks, &c., who suffer from anæmia, likewise stokers on board ship and sailors employed entirely between decks or in the hold of a vessel, where the amount of sunlight is necessarily very limited or perhaps entirely absent; these men, if contrasted with the workers on the upper deck, compare very unfavorably in their healthful appearance, although, as regards diet and sea air, some of them are very nearly under the same conditions. Referring again to Arctic experiences, there is every reason to expect the converse of the depressing influence exercised by the prolonged and intense darkness of the Arctic night.

Dr W. Hammond contributed a paper in the 'Medico-Chirurgical Transactions,' on the influence of light, showing that the development of tadpoles may be retarded by depriving them of light, and that in an experiment with two kittens, where one was confined in a dark box and the other in a box to which light was admitted, the weight was perceptibly increased by light, while the growth of the other was retarded.

Other experiments with which we are familiar are mentioned in the paper, and tend to demonstrate that the action of light is of benefit in many conditions, anæmia, chlorosis, and phthisis, being among the number.

The hæmatinic properties of iron we know to be enhanced by sunlight.

In the examples of the prevalence of anæmia through the absence of sufficient sunlight, other factors enter largely into the cause of that disease; but the want of sunlight bears on it very strongly.

The aspect of health which is created by the sun's rays speaks for itself as being a therapeutic agent of more or less value.

At altitudes of 5000 feet in Switzerland, the sun radiation is very powerful, and the numerous bright days throughout the winter allow of frequent exposure to the direct and reflected rays of the sun.

In any subtropical climate a "sunning" in this manner, would be injudicious if not attended with some danger; in fact, the oppression and discomfort felt in a warm climate deter one from seeking the sunlight and induce a languid desire for shade.

CHAPTER VI

BAROMETRIC PRESSURE—OXYGEN AND OZONE

In approaching the subject of barometric pressure it will be interesting to first quote the experiences of Glaisher, Gay Lussac, and others, of its result on the action of the pulse and respiration.

Balloon ascents of	Feet.	Increase in Pulse.
Biot and Gay Lussac	9,000	18 to 30
Glaisher	17,000	10 to 24
	24,000	24 to 31

An ascent by Glaisher and Coxwell on the 17th July, 1862, gave these results:

Mr Glaisher's pulse	76
Mr Coxwell's pulse	74
At 17,000 feet, Glaisher	100
„ „ Coxwell	84

	21st August at 1000 feet.	At 11,000.
Mr Coxwell	95	90
Mr Inglelow	80	100
Captain Percival	90	88

The humidity of the air was found to decrease with the height in a wonderfully decreasing ratio, till at heights exceeding five miles the amount of aqueous vapour in the atmosphere was found to be very small indeed.[1]

The number of pulsations usually increased with elevation as also the number of respirations.[2]

Armieux in the case of eighty-six invalids removed from the plains to Barèges at a height of 4000 feet, satisfied himself, after a residence of four months, the respirations were increased by two, and the beats of the pulse reduced by four.

He also found on careful examination that the eighty-six men had in four months gained on an average one inch in girth round the chest.

Dr Kellett found that the invalids at Landour gained one inch chiefly during the first two weeks.[3]

Jourdanet has asserted ('Du Mexique,' p.

[1] 'Lectures in Exeter Hall,' by Glaisher.
[2] 'Glaisher's Travels in the Air.' 1871.
[3] 'M. R.,' vol. lviii, 1876.

76) that the usual notion that the respirations are augmented in number in the inhabitants of high lands is "completely erroneous; that the respirations are in fact lessened, and that from time to time a deeper inspiration is voluntarily made as partial compensation."

But Coindet from 1500 observations on French and Mexicans does not confirm this.

The mean number of respirations was

  19·36 per minute for the French,
  20·297 „ „ Mexicans.
            Parkes.

From these and more recent observations, evidence is in favour of a slight increase both in the pulse and respirations in persons first dwelling at high altitudes, but the length of time these phenomena last has not been noted with much accuracy.

It must not be forgotten, however, that the increase in the measurements of the chest, and the excursions forward of the sternum, after a short residence in Alpine valleys, may also in a great measure be explained by the gain in flesh and strength, for we know that on convalescence from many diseases at *low* altitudes this event is a consequence of returning health and a token of general improvement.

The difference in the amount of oxygen inhaled at an ascent of 5000 feet is as follows. In a cubic foot of dry air at 32° Fahr. and 30 inches barometric pressure, we find 130·375 grains of oxygen.

A man draws on an average, when tranquil, 16·6 cubic feet of air into his lungs per hour, $130·375 \times 16·6 = 2164·2$ grains of oxygen.

An ascent of 5000 feet, which reduces the barometer to 25 inches, gives 108·6 grains of oxygen in a cubic foot of dry air at 32° (Parkes).

Without allowing for a slight difference of oxygen at high altitudes, owing to the small amount of moisture in the air, and also to the lowness of temperature, about three additional respirations per minute would be necessary to compensate for a barometric fall of five inches, but by experiments on animals it has been found that as long as the percentage of oxygen was not below 14, the same quantity was absorbed into the blood as when this gas was in normal proportion.

The quantity of oxygen in the atmosphere surrounding animals appears to have very little influence on the amount of this gas absorbed by them, for the quantity consumed is not greater, even though an excess of oxygen be added to the atmosphere experimented with (Regnault and Reiset).

It therefore does not seem at all probable that the lessened *weight* of oxygen taken into the lungs, when breathing rarefied air at 5000 feet, necessitates any increase in the number of respirations.

This is by no means unworthy of notice when we reflect that in all forms of phthisis there is diminished respiratory function.

The explanation why breathing mountain air should increase the number of respirations and expand the lungs cannot be satisfactorily accounted for by the laws of mechanical pressure, as the diminution is everywhere the same, both internally and externally, and such an equilibrium of force being established disposes of any theory which attributes a freedom of the circulation, or increased thoracic capacity, directly to diminished barometric pressure.

The rhythm of the involuntary movements of the chest-walls and diaphragm depend entirely on nervous influence, and it would appear that the cause of extended respiratory movements depends on the excitation of the respiratory centres, influenced, amongst other causes, by certain fibres which run in the course of the pneumogastric. Rarefied air irritating these fibres would therefore account for the additional number of respirations and extended chest-movements. An increased proportion of blood in the lungs would also tend to this result.

In the cold high altitudes we may, then, attribute the change to both these causes, but whether this phenomenon occurs in persons whose lungs are already quickened in action by disease is a matter for observation. In these cases the exciting cause of respiratory rhythm depends more on the proportion of carbonic acid and oxygen in the blood than on the density of the air breathed.

The following facts prove that this condition of the blood influences the respiratory movements :—1. The respiratory movements can be totally arrested if, either by a forced artificial respiration (by blowing air into the lungs) or by forced voluntary breathing, the blood becomes saturated with oxygen and poor in carbonic acid ("apnœa"). 2. Respiration becomes stronger, and the more accessory muscles take part in it ("dyspnœa"). The poorer in oxygen and the richer in carbonic acid the blood is, as, *e. g.* on the entrance of air or fluid into the pleural cavities, causing a collapse of the lung, or when, by inflammation, &c., the lungs are unfit for respiration ('Herman's Physiology').

There are three causes at high altitudes which advance the combination of the carbon and hydrogen of the body with the oxygen of the air, viz. cold air, sunlight, and lessened pressure; therefore, it is conceivable that the additional weight of oxygen absorbed by the blood does not become such an overplus as would, when reaching the medulla, induce a tendency to apnœa, but may be sufficient to exert some inhibitory influence and balance irritation of the peripheral fibres of the pneumogastric in the lungs. Or, to summarise thus :

1. Rarefied air and larger proportion of blood in the lungs, increasing respiration.

2. Oxygen in blood circulating to medulla, retarding respiration.

The balance being a little in favour of No. 1 in healthy persons; but in impaired lungs with quickened action (owing to excess of carbonic acid in the blood) the increased quantity of oxygen absorbed by the blood at high levels seems to have a proportionately stronger inhibitory influence. This is borne out by the fact of many patients breathing comparatively freely when leaving the plains who again experience dyspnœa on their return from the mountains.

From the experiments of Dr Marcet at high altitudes in Switzerland and the Island of Teneriffe, it appears that more air in bulk, but less in weight, is breathed at high altitudes, and that a larger proportion of carbonic acid is excreted in the cold altitudes of Switzerland.

At Teneriffe the carbonic acid was not increased in amount, whereas in the Swiss altitudes of 13,000 feet an increase of 15 per cent. was discovered.

We can attribute this to the lower temperature of the latter country (as Dr Marcet observes), and also to the larger amount of sunlight, and in a *cold* high climate there would be a greater volume of blood in the lungs to avail itself of the absorption of the oxygen.

One may be said to live quickly at these altitudes. As pointed out in Chapter IV, the most perfect health is maintained by a rapid waste and repair of the tissues of the body. This increased combustion does not mean shortened existence, but improved health, provided that repair and loss are equally balanced.

Theoretically, lungs which would be incapable of performing the respiratory functions completely at sea-level would, on the patient rising to higher cold levels, utilise more oxygen in proportion to the weight of the air inhaled the higher they ascend, within ordinary limits.

Although, perhaps, not quite so much fresh air is breathed in a cold climate by those who sleep with closed windows as is breathed in the warmer health resorts by persons who sleep with windows open, the three conditions of excessive sunlight, cold atmosphere, and lessened barometric pressure, may partly compensate for any advantage in that respect. Indeed, it is difficult anywhere to persuade many patients to ventilate their rooms at night.

Little can be said on the subject of ozone. Dr Fox, in a work on 'Ozone and Antozone,' remarks of the former that it is nature's great deodorising and purifying principle, and that there is reason to suppose that ozone is absorbed by the blood-corpuscles with great rapidity. It would be unnecessary to mention the numerous statements of the properties and effects of this body; some conflicting, and others of not much bearing on the subject of climate. One thing seems certain, that ozone is found to be more abundant in healthy localities than in large towns, or where decomposing substances are present.

Dr Sanderson has observed large quantities of ozone at Geneva and Chamouny; and as this body is found in pure country air and in mountainous districts, we may be satisfied of its presence in the high Swiss valleys surrounded by pine forests; but the benefits derived from a residence near pine trees may, perhaps, be due, to some extent, to the direct influence of the turpentine diffused through the air.

CHAPTER VII

METEOROLOGICAL CONDITIONS AT HIGH ALTITUDES, AND THEIR EFFECTS ON THE LUNGS. THE THERMOMETER AND THE SENSATION OF COLD.

In the following list climatic conditions are noted in what may be considered the order of importance with regard to health:

1. Dryness of the atmosphere and its comparative freedom from mechanical irritants, germs, and noxious gases.
2. Profusion of sunlight with a low temperature.
3. Absence of high winds.
4. Diminished barometric pressure.

There is nothing to create a necessity of attaching undue weight to the value of any one of these features of climate; they must be taken collectively for consideration, although, if one deserves more prominence than another, it is the absence of impurities in the air; but other circumstances are closely associated with this. For instance, if this so-called pure air were accompanied with high winds persons would not avail themselves of out-door exercise, and if the humidity of this air were in excess catarrhs and chills would result.

The physiological results, on pulmonary complaints, of the conditions enumerated, may be stated thus:

1. Lessened irritation of the respiratory tract from absence of dust.

2. Evaporation of morbid secretions in the lungs, promoted by reduced barometric pressure and dryness of the atmosphere.

3. Increased oxidation of blood and tissue from sunlight, cold air, and reduced pressure.

4. Increased quantity of blood circulating in the lungs, caused by the low temperature, the freedom of the circulation being aided by extended chest movements.

5. Increased activity in the pulmonary lymphatics (depending on circulation and expansion), and a general improvement in nutrition, with diminished liability to attacks

of bronchitis and catarrh, also an exhilarating effect on the brain and nervous system.

The sleeplessness induced by lessened barometric pressure seems to indicate either a larger supply of blood to the cerebrum than at low levels, or increased oxidation of blood circulating in the brain. The excitation sometimes experienced on a sudden rise in altitude is in favour of the latter supposition.

What seems at first a drawback to Alpine localities as health resorts is the lowness of the temperature during winter. Although the thermometer minutely registers the effects of heat or cold on mercury, alcohol, &c., it is by no means a reliable index to the sensations or effects on the animal frame of surrounding air temperature.

The thermometer has formerly been made the basis for too arbitrary decisions as to what should be the height of the mercury in climates suitable for phthisis; some writers even confined themselves within limitations of a dozen degrees or so. Other conditions are so intimately connected with temperature in producing sensations of warmth or cold, that temperature, considered alone, becomes extremely misleading.

It is not unusual for a person to feel intensely cold at 40° Fahr. in some localities, whilst in other places he might be comfortably warm, sitting in the open air, at 20° or 25°. Such a wide difference as 15° or 20° producing the opposite sensation we should expect, cautions us not to be too arbitrary in condemning or extolling a health resort on the score of actual temperature, remembering that it is only a factor of other important conditions, and within certain limits is less powerful in causing impressions of cold or heat than either wind or dampness.

The peculiarly sheltered positions of some of the high valleys in Switzerland, the stillness of the air, low percentage of watery vapour, and great amount of sun radiation, enable low temperatures to be borne with comfort.

When the snow melting begins it is advisable for patients to quit these places, to escape the bad consequences of a universal thaw. Some leave 30° or 40° Fahr. to shiver and contract colds at 50°. This has happened to cases leaving Davos, where a change to a place many degrees higher in temperature has caused feelings of actual chilliness.

It is not for a moment implied that climatic conditions, grateful at all times in health and disease, are not found in certain localities, where the range of the thermometer is generally from 50° to 65°, or thereabouts. This equality of temperature with dryness, &c., enables patients to be constantly in the open air, and, if not out of the house, to be able to avail themselves of a system of "hyperventilation" day and night; but, on the other hand, it is now well known that other places can be found as favorable for early phthisis, if not more so, in cold climates, although the range of the thermometer is not so limited.

Variations at a low temperature with still air do not produce the discomfort that many would suppose. A fall of 5° or 6° is often imperceptible, which is not the case with high temperatures, as such a rise or fall at 60° Fahr. would be more easily detected.

Perhaps this may be accounted for by the warmer air containing more watery vapour.

A freezing temperature in England, with dampness and wind, is more pinching to the frame, painful to the air passages and parts exposed, than a still dry atmosphere of an Alpine height in winter, where the thermometer may bo at 15 or 20 degrees.

It has been frequently asserted by Canadians who have wintered in England that they have felt the atmosphere to be more disagreeable and apparently colder to their subjective sensations, than the low temperatures of tho Canadian winter.

This has been the author's experience of winters in Canada and Nova Scotia, where phthisis does well during the dry cold, but badly when the early spring thaw sets in.

Similar results have been obtained at Davos ; for information on these points we must principally rely on our own physicians at home, who recommend cases there, and have opportunities of again seeing their condition on returning.

The statements published have, so far,

been very encouraging; but it is undeniable that some patients visit Davos who ought never to have left England, if even for a southern clime, and, what is still more unfortunate, do not quit the place until travelling becomes a positive danger.

The discomfort of the stone-heated rooms has been greatly over-estimated. These porcelain and stone stoves are seldom so hot that the bare hand cannot be placed on them; they are lighted two or three times daily with a few pieces of wood, and allowed to burn out each time. The large size of the stove retains a quantity of heat, which is slowly radiated into the room.

Undue dryness of the atmosphere, produced by the warm air, may easily be neutralised by having a vessel containing water on or near the stove, though the air seldom becomes so dry as to require this.

When having a large and well distributed supply of warming arrangements, external air may be allowed to enter a building more freely than with a limited number of hot stoves; and the pernicious condition of "confinement in a stove-heated apartment," is changed into a comfortably warmed and fresh atmosphere.

In conclusion, it must be remarked that a "suitable climate" is only one restorative agent, and that other remedies and precautions are not only indispensable but become of greater value in the hands of the physician, and more potent in their effects on disease.

The late Dr Tanner observes :—"Notwithstanding the excellent writings of Sir James Clark, Edwin Lee, Granville, Burgess, Alexander Taylor, D. J. T. Francis, Scoresby, Jackson, and others, many invalids migrate every autumn to the South of France, Italy, Spain, &c., merely to find a grave.

This happens partly because cases of far advanced disease are still sent abroad when they ought to be kept at home, partly because a situation unfavorable to the particular malady is selected, the laws of climate being ill understood ; and in some measure, because it is difficult to persuade the sick that simple change to another country is only one of the means by which they are to regain health. For although there can be no doubt that in change of air physicians have an efficient remedial agent, yet it is certain that this remedy, like all others, is not of indiscriminate application, but must be prescribed with judgment and discretion.[1]

[1] 'Tanner's Index of Diseases,' by Dr. Broadbent.

CHAPTER VIII

THE DRAWBACKS OF DAVOS

ANY remarks on the climate of Switzerland would be incomplete without reference being made to the Föhn wind.[1] The altitude and low temperature of Davos modify, to some extent, the disagreeable qualities of this wind.

[1] Dr Wild says, the Föhn as such is known only in the north-eastern valleys of Switzerland (1), and it is there distinguished by its great heat and still more by its peculiar dryness before which the snow disappears both by rapid melting and also by that rapid evaporation which has obtained for it the appropriate name of the snow-eater (Schneefresser).

But while the Föhn proper is blowing in the valleys of the north-east eating away the snow in winter, or in summer and autumn drying the hay or ripening the grapes, over the south-west of Switzerland a warm and wet wind blows, which precipitates its moisture in a heavy down-pour and floods the country with rain and melted snow (1). The distinctly Föhn stations named by Dr Wild are, Glarus, Auen, Altdorf, Engelberg, Schwyz, Chur, and Klosters.

The nearest Föhn station is Klosters, which is 1700 feet below. Nevertheless the wind frequently makes its presence felt and mars the full benefits of the winter season, as in the winter of 1878, and the greater part of last winter, during which, rises in temperature with dampness, limited the number of enjoyable days, and gave rise to the dangers of contracting catarrh or bronchitis.

Happily these winters are infrequent.

It must not bo forgotten by those who seek health in the Alps that a residence there will become somewhat dull, without settled employment for leisure hours. At Davos there are facilities for acquiring a knowledge of languages; amusements in the way of music, theatrical entertainments, &c., in the hotels, billiard and reading rooms, skating and tobogging out of doors, pleasant walks, seats and shelters not being found wanting.

Perhaps it is not to be regretted that there is an absence of picture galleries, museums, or cold churches to attract the visits of patients fond of sight seeing.

On the other hand the exhilarating effects of the sun and mountain air make up to a great extent for the deficiency in amusements; and with the majority of visitors time does not seem to drag heavily, energy is increased, and there appears to be no dejection of mind; the latter a very important consideration in the treatment of pulmonary phthisis.

In mentioning Davos as a health-resort, it must be remembered that there are many high valleys in Switzerland, equal to, if not exceeding that locality in health-giving meteorological conditions. The position of Weisen is well situated; at present Davos possesses the name and reputation of a sanatorium; but it appears likely to become overcrowded, and the benefits then of living among a sparse population in scattered dwellings will be modified by the drawbacks of dwelling in a closely built village, which change seems slowly but surely approaching.

The emptying of cesspools and accumulations of manure from the cow sheds, &c.,

during the autumn months, for manuring the grass preparatory to the snow fall, is a nuisance which requires serious attention; and it is a matter of regret that the inhabitants still adopt a system of drainage conducted on such primitive principles.

Greater attention might be paid to sanitary arrangements within and without the hotels, and some general satisfactory plan of ventilation might be adopted.

An important consideration in sending cases to these altitudes is that too sudden a rise from a low level is likely to produce unpleasant symptoms occasionally; this may be obviated in a measure, by a residence at half the altitude, if possible; for instance, in the selection of Davos or Weisen, as a winter resort, a stay of a week at Chur (2000 feet) would be very desirable, and in many cases the only means which seems likely to enable sensitive persons to resist these attacks.[1]

---

[1] 'The author's own case was reported in the ' Brit. Med. Journal' of the 19th November, 1880.

THE DRAWBACKS OF DAVOS 51

It should be clearly understood by patients recommended to these places, that they go there for health and not for pleasure. Before the end of four months, the life becomes monotonous, and unless one has some settled employment for leisure hours, and for the days spent in-doors on account of bad weather, tediousness and *ennui* will be occasionally experienced.

Although food is good and plentiful, the meal times are not suited for invalids. If possible delicate persons should be trained to make a good breakfast, an afternoon dinner, and a lighter but substantial meal in the evening.

Breakfast in Switzerland simply consists of bread and butter with honey,[1] tea or coffee, then at 12 or 1 a good lunch with soup and meats is taken, and dinner laid at 5.30 or 6 p.m., the majority retiring to rest about 9 o'clock.

From this it is obvious that most of the digestion takes place between the hours of

---

[1] At most of the hotels in Switzerland "Honey" is a compound of glycerine, syrup, &c.

1 and 8 p.m., the stomach during sixteen hours having very little occupation, except with liquids, perhaps.

Although the habit can bo easily acquired of such a division of meals, it is not desirable that the work of digestion should be so irregularly distributed over the twenty-four hours. A better arrangement would not interfere with the milk drinking, &c.

As in the case of change of air to milder climates, the beneficial effects on early disease are more marked in proportion as the disease is less developed. Some few advanced cases have done well, but, as a rule, the cold is too severe for the class of pulmonary complaints generally described by the term "advanced."

Many deaths have occurred from the inability of feeble patients to withstand the cold of the bad weather, although on the damp and windy days the temperature is generally higher than during the periods of calmness and sunshine; however, on the former occasions those enemies to comfort, wind and moisture, produce ill effects.

Frequently persons, whose lungs are seriously diseased, live under the most unfavorable conditions, with insufficient food and clothing, combined with exposure to the inclemency of the English winter. Many such die in harness, working to within a few days of their death; consequently it is quite conceivable that grave cases can exist, and perhaps improve a little, in an Alpine climate; but there is no doubt that a mild country, with a constant supply of clean air indoors day and night, is the best condition for advanced phthisis.

The nearer the approach to health the greater is the benefit derived from the bracing and invigorating effects of cold, dry regions, and the result on a debilitated European of a change of air to such places is of more value, and is more lasting, than that of a warm or mild climate.

In regard to phthisis, there appears to be a limit, difficult of definition, where cold resorts cease to be of value, as " change," and even become dangerous. No definite lines can be laid down in describing this; consideration must be taken of age, vigour, digestion, heart's action, and ordinary powers of resistance to cold, as well as the state of local disease.

The reports which originate from Davos of extraordinary cures of pulmonary complaints, are in no way surprising, except as regards their number, for occasionally phthisis is seen to mend in an almost unlooked-for manner; but the universal recommendation of the place for all cases fit to leave their homes is not only not attended with universal satisfaction, but is in the highest degree reckless and dangerous.

We have not only to consider the low temperatures, with sunlight and calm air, which the most delicate persons can bear with a sense of enjoyment and comfort, but the introduction to the winter, with its frequent changes, attended with rain, snow, fog, &c., must not be forgotten. In no case does this ever approach the prolonged dampness and discomfort of English weather, still, it is not all sunshine.

It is misleading and cruel to make too

light of this, and most essential in the recommendation of foreign health-resorts that their disadvantages be clearly stated, as well as the probable benefits likely to accrue to persons visiting these places. Much disappointment is thereby averted, and many, who otherwise would expect impossibilities, do not become discontented.

WEATHER REPORTS FOR 1880.

12th October, 9 a.m.—Cloudy with slight sunshine; wind east; maximum thermometer 42, minimum 35; barometer, 25·20.

10 a.m.—Raining; foggy overhead; dry bulb 35, wet 33.

5 p.m.—Dry bulb 36, wet 34; snowing since 11 a.m.; cold and disagreeable day; wind east, 1 to 3.

13th, 9 a.m.—Wind north-east, 1; bright sun, blue sky with a few clouds; max. 42, min. 20; fine morning with the exception of the thaw; dry bulb 39, wet 35; bar. 25·02.

3 p.m.—Dry bulb 44, wet 40 ; wind northeast, increasing to 3 ; clouds away to the north-east, near the earth.

5 p.m.—max. 46, min. 37 ; dry bulb 38, wet 35.

14th, 9 a.m.—Foggy and overcast; wind north-east, 2 ; max. 43 ; min. 33 ; dry bulb 37, wet 34; snow almost disappeared from valley; bar. 25·60.

10 a.m.—Wind increased to 4; fog surrounding the hills; blue sky perceptible; slight sunshine between passing clouds.

3 p.m.—Wind 3 to 4, north; less fog; roads dry; wet bulb 37, dry 41 ; max. 42, min. 35.

15th.—Wind 0 ; dry bulb 33, wet 29 ; max. 40, min. 25 ; bar. 25·60 ; clear blue sky, bright sun, dry underfoot.

10.30.—Dry bulb 41, wet 35.

2.30 p.m.—Dry bulb 50, wet 40.

4.30 p.m.—Max. 52, min. 40 ; dry bulb 43, wet 36. Fine day with plenty of sunshine.

16th, 9 a.m.—Max. 42, min. 25 ; dry bulb 41, wet 35; bar. 25·47 ; blue sky ; wind 0 ; bright sun.

3 p.m.—Max. 58, min. 30; dry bulb 51, wet 45; overcast. Fairly good day with occasional sunshine.

17th, 9 a.m.—Max. 48, min. 32; dry bulb 49, wet 43; bar. 25·47; rather cloudy, blue sky seen between packs of cirro-cumulus; wind south-west; overhead calm in valley.

3 p.m.—Max. 57, min. 43; dry bulb 50, wet 44; overcast at north end of valley; wind east, 4. Fair day until 2.30 p.m.

18th.—Max. 50, min. 35; dry bulb 50, wet 45; bar. 25·45; dull appearance of sky, no sun visible; wind east, 3; roads dry.

3 p.m.—Dry bulb 47, wet 45; max. 50, min. 40; fog over north end of valley; no blue sky anywhere to be seen.

19th.—Max. 46, min. 43; dry bulb 45, wet 43; bar. 25·34; rained during the night, a slight drizzle continues; clouds around valley and among the pine trees; at 11 a.m. spaces of blue sky became visible and the sun appeared. Dry bulb 51, wet 46; damp under foot; wind north-east, 2 to 3.

3 p.m.—Packs of clouds floating down

the north end of valley; warm sunshine; max. 50, min. 49; dry bulb 45, wet 43.

4 p.m.—Fog filling the whole valley; dry bulb 42, wet 41; wind east, 3; bar. 25·29. Bad day; three hours' sunshine.

20th.—Max. 44, min. 39; dry bulb 44, wet 42; bar. 25·18; blue sky with scattered clouds of cirrus; sunshine.

Noon.—Wind south, 2 (Föhn).

5 p.m.—Max. 56, min. 37; dry bulb 48, wet 42; bar. 25·10; sunshine for three or four hours. Fair day for persons walking.

21st.—Max. 50, min. 39; dry bulb 52, wet 50; bar. 25·11; overcast; wind south, 2 (Föhn).

4 p.m.—Max. 52, min. 46; dry bulb 47, wet 46. Dull and cloudy day; patches of fog on slopes; no sunshine.

22nd.—Max. 54, min. 42; dry bulb 54; wet 53; wind south, 2 (Föhn); overcast and cloudy.

Noon.—Max. 59, min. 52; dry bulb 59, wet 53; cloudy overhead, clouds high.

5 p.m.—Slight rain.

23rd.—Max. 46, min. 40; dry bulb 45, wet 43; bar. 25·23; Föhn wind; drizzling rain; fog on slopes; sunshine at noon.

3 p.m.—Max. 55, min. 45; dry bulb 50, wet 45; sunshine continues.

24th.—Max. 50, min. 34; dry bulb 35, wet 34; bar. 25·18; moist snow falling, roads muddy; wind north-east, 2.

Noon.—Wind north-east, 4; moist snow still falling; dry bulb 36, wet 34.

3 p.m.—Cloudy, a little blue sky seen; max. 39, min. 36; dry bulb 37, wet 34; bar. 25·23; wind east, 3.

25th.—Max. 39, min. 26; dry bulb 29, wet 27; bar. 25·33; wind 3 to 4; has been blowing all night; clouds over slopes at north end of valley; blue sky with packs of clouds (cirrus); sunshine; roads hard from last night's frost.

3 p.m.—Max. 34, min. 32; dry bulb 33, wet 32; wind east, 2.

26th.—Max. 29, min. 20; dry bulb 31, wet 29; bar. 25·25; wind 0; blue sky and sunshine.

11 a.m.—Dry bulb 42, wet 33.

3 p.m.—Dry bulb 46, wet 36; max. 50, min. 45.

27th.—Max. 46, min. 33; dry bulb 47,

wet 45; bar. 25·19; wind south-west, 1 (Föhn); cloudy, with gleams of sunshine.

3 p.m.—Raining; dry bulb 47, wet 45.

28th.—Max. 50, min. 40; dry bulb 45, wet 43; bar. 25·11; wind south 1 (Föhn); cirro-cumulus packs of clouds and blue sky; snow entirely disappeared, except on the summits of the Alps.

Noon.—Dry bulb 53, wet 46; Föhn wind, sunlight, and blue sky; clouds approaching from the south.

29th.—Max. 52, min. 40; dry bulb 44 wet 43; bar. 24·92; wind south, 3 (Föhn); packs of clouds with blue sky.

Noon.—Dry bulb 41½, wet 41; valley filled with fog; wind north-east, 2; sky clearing.

1 p.m.—Fog clearing; Föhn wind overhead, north wind in valley.

5 p.m.—Dry bulb 34¼, wet 34. Very bad day.

30th.—Max. 36, min. 25; dry bulb 27, wet 27; bar. 25·09; wind north, 4; overcast, snowing.

Noon.—Dry bulb 30, wet 28.

3 p.m.—Max. 32, min. 24; dry bulb 30,

wet 29; sunshine since 1 p.m; wind northeast, 2; calm in valley. Bad day.
31st.—Max. 26, min. 12; dry bulb 21, frozen; bar. 25·28; sunshine and blue sky.
4 p.m.—Max. 34, min. 11. Fine day, wind north, 0 to 2.
1st November.—Max. 24, min. 13; bar. 25·28.
3 p.m.—Max. 30, min. 20; wind 2 and 3, north-east. Rather windy day, but bright sunshine with blue sky.
2nd.—Max. 28, min. 18; bar. 25·26; wind south, 2 to 3 (Föhn). North wind blowing at 4 p.m.
3rd.—Max. 34, min. 28; bar. 25·09; wind south (Föhn); overcast.
3 p.m.—Max. 36, min. 32. Bad day.
4th.—Max. 34, min. 25; bar. 25·06; Föhn wind, 3 overhead, 1 in the valley; blue sky and occasional sunshine; snow fell during the night, two inches.
1 p.m.—Dry bulb 44, wet 39; snow almost disappeared. Fair day.
5th.—Max. 44, min. 28; dry bulb 31,

wet 30; bar. 25·23; wind south-east, 1; foggy and overcast.

3 p.m.—Slight fall of snow; dry bulb 33, wet 32½; Föhn wind low. Bad day.

6th.—Max. 32, min. 27; dry bulb 32, wet 31; bar. 25·42; fog on the slopes; overcast.

3 p.m.—Sunshine for two hours; Föhn wind higher; dry bulb 37, wet 35; max. 28, min. 35.

7th.—Max. 32, min. 20; bar. 25·45; blue sky and sunshine.

1 p.m.—Dry bulb 46, wet 38; no wind. Fine day.

8th.—Max. 40, min. 27; dry bulb 39, wet 34; bar. 25·40; wind south, 3 overhead, 1 in valley (Föhn); blue sky covered with cirro-cumulus; glimpses of sunshine.

1 p.m.—Rain; max. 42, min. 41.

3 p.m.—Max. 50, min. 40; dry bulb 48, wet 48. Bad day.

9th.—Max. 50, min. 37; dry bulb 36½, wet 36; bar. 25·31; Föhn wind; rain during the night; foggy; clearing at noon.

2 p.m.—Cloudy, with sunshine and blue sky; dry bulb 45, wet 43.

4 p.m.—Dry bulb 40, wet 39; dense fog in the evening, hygrometer showing saturation. Very bad day.

10th.—Max. 41, min. 32; dry bulb $34\frac{1}{2}$, wet 34; bar. 25·31; wind south, 1 (Fohn); foggy.

Noon.—Wind 2 in the valley, north.

3 p.m.—Max. 39, min. 32; dry bulb 35, wet 33; wind westerly (high), north-east, low.

5 p.m.—Dry bulb $32\frac{1}{2}$, wet 32. Very bad day.

11th.—Max. 34, min. 19; dry bulb 27, wet 26; bar. 25·40; wind 0; blue sky and sunshine; clouds of cirro-stratus to north end of valley.

3 p.m.—Dry bulb 41, wet 35; max. 44, min. 24. Good day, with the exception of damp roads in the afternoon.

12th.—Max. 40, min. 21; dry bulb 26, wet 25; bar. 25·39; clear blue sky; no wind.

3 p.m.—Dry bulb 35, wet 32; thick fog in the evening. Fair day.

13th.—Max. 36, min. 19; dry bulb 36, wet 33; bar. 25·40; wind west, 2; cloudy.

11 a.m.—Foggy; dry bulb 41, wet 39.

3 p.m.—Dry bulb 40, wet 39; max. 44, min. 33. Very bad day.

14th.—Max. 42, min. 31; dry bulb 38½, wet 38; bar. 25·34; wind 0; blue sky, with cirro-stratus.

3 p.m.—Dry bulb 47, wet 40; max. 53, min. 32. Fine day.

15th.—Max. 48, min. 27; bar. 25·15; wind north-east, 1 in valley, Föhn overhead; blue sky, with scattered patches of cirrus.

3 p.m.—Max. 48, min. 37; dry bulb 41, wet 38; wind south-west-west in valley; sunshine to 1.30 p.m. Fine day to 1.30, bad after.

16th.—Max. 40, min. 27; dry bulb 35, wet 32; bar. 25·12; wind west, gusty; blue sky to be seen between clouds.

3 p.m.—Föhn wind; dry bulb 46, wet 37; cloudy. Bad day.

17th.—Max. 48, min. 32; dry bulb 35, wet 34; bar. 24·76; wind, 1 to 2 south-west; overcast and foggy; rain and snow.

Noon.—Hygrometer showed saturation.

3 p.m.—Snowing; max. 40, min. 30. Bad day.

18th.—Max. 32, min. 25; dry bulb 26, wet frozen; bar. 24·82; wind north-east, 2 overhead, calm in valley; blue sky; sunshine.

3 p.m.—Max. 34, min. 23. Fine day.

19th.—Max. 32, min. 12; bar. 24·83; wind south-west (Föhn); two hours' sunshine in the morning.

3 p.m.—Max. 40, min. 30; dry bulb 41, wet 38. Fair day.

20th.—Max. 38, min. 26; bar. 25·12; wind south-west (Föhn).

3 p.m.—Max. 38, min. 28; dry bulb 33, wet 32; wind south-west-west; clouds high. Fair day.

21st.—Max. 34, min. 24; bar. 25·23; wind south-west, 1.

3 p.m.—Dry bulb 39, wet 33; max. 42, min. 24; overcast; snowing in the evening. Fair day.

22nd.—Max. 40, min. 32; dry bulb 35½, wet 35; overcast; no wind.

3 p.m.—Wind south, 1; misty on slopes. Bad day.

23rd.—Max. 40, min. 18; bar. 25·28; wind south; blue sky with clouds.

3 p.m.—Max. 36, min. 27. Fine day.

24th.—Max. 30, min. 18; bar. 25·48; wind 0; clear blue sky, sunshine. Fine day.

25th.—Max. 38, min. 22; bar. 25·45; wind west, 1; clear blue sky, sunshine.

3 p.m.—Max. 40, min. 31; dry bulb 37, wet 34. Fine day.

26th.—Max. 40, min. 25; bar. 25·51; wind west, 1.

3 p.m.—Max. 46, min. 30; dry bulb 40, wet 37; cloudy afternoon. Moderately fine day.

27th.—Max. 45, min. 29; dry bulb 34; wet 32; bar. 25·44; wind west, 1; blue sky seen.

3 p.m.—Max. 46, min. 33. Fair day.

28th.—Max. 40, min. 32; dry bulb 35, wet 34; wind 0; bar. 25·63; sunshine.

3 p.m.—Max. 40, min. 34; wind southwest, 1; dull sky; foggy in the evening. Fair day.

29th.—Max. 36, min. 24; dry bulb 29, wet 27; bar. 25·65; wind 0; clear blue sky. Fine day.

30th.—Max. 40, min. 23; bar. 25·68; wind 0; clear blue sky.

3 p.m.—Dry bulb 34, wet 31. Fine day.

1st December.—Max. 34, min. 23 ; bar.
25·53 ; wind 0 ; blue sky and plenty of sun.
3 p.m.—Dry bulb 37, wet 33 ; max. 40,
min. 27. Fine day.
2nd.—Max. 36, min. 19 ; bar. 25·45 ;
wind 0.
3 p.m.—Max. 36, min. 22 ; blue sky.
Fine day.
3rd.—Max. 34, min. 17 ; bar. 25·47 ;
wind 0.
3 p.m.—Max. 34, min. 23; clear blue sky.
Fine day.
4th. — Max. 34, min. 18 ; bar. 25.52 ;
wind 0.
3 p.m.—Max. 42, min. 24 ; blue sky with
cirrus. Fine day.
5th.—Max. 34, min. 21 ; bar. 25·59; wind
north, 1.
3 p.m.—Max. 32, min. 23 ; blue sky.
Fine day.
6th.—Max. 32, min. 24 ; bar. 25·60 ; wind
west, 2 ; overcast.
3 p.m.—Max. 38, min. 30 ; fine after 11
a.m. Fair day.
7th.—Max. 34, min. 31 ; bar. 25·64 ; dry

bulb 35, wet 34½; wind 1 (Thalwind); no sky to be seen; snowing.

3 p.m.—Max. 40, min. 32; foggy. Bad day.

8th.—Max. 37, min. 21; bar. 25·73; wind north-east, 1; blue sky with clouds.

3 p.m.—Max. 38, min. 23. Fair day.

9th.—Max. 32, min. 20; bar. 25·56; wind west, 1; cloudy.

3 p.m.—Max. 40, min. 26; hygrometer showed saturation; snowing; wind 0. Bad day.

10th.—Max. 41, min. 29; bar. 25·39; wind 0; sun appearing at 1 p.m.

3 p.m.—Thalwind north-east, 2 to 5, gusty; snow blowing about like smoke. Bad day.

11th.—Max. 41, min. 29; bar. 25·42; wind 0; no sky to be seen; cloudy.

3 p.m.—Snowing slightly; max. 38, min. 29. Fair day.

12th.—Max. 30, min. 12; bar. 25·38; wind half north-east, ½; blue sky with dark clouds.

3 p.m.—Wind south-east, 1; max. 30, min. 22; clear blue sky and moderate sunshine. Fine day.

13th.—Max. 31, min. 15; bar. 25·31; wind 0; overcast.

3 p.m.—Max. 32, min. 29; snowing. Bad day.

14th.—Max. 40, min. 21; bar. 25·25; wind 0; snowing most of the day. Bad day.

15th.—Max. 35, min. 28; bar. 25·19; wind 0.

3 p.m.—Max. 36, min. 33; wind half westerly; snowing; dense fog in valley at 5 p.m. Bad day.

16th.—Max. 34, min. 13; bar. 25·12; wind 0; snowing; fog in the valley.

3 p.m.—Max. 40, min. 28; still foggy; blue sky; sun occasionally. Bad day

17th.—Max. 32, min. 21; bar. 25·02; wind west, 1; overcast; foggy.

3 p.m.—Max. 40, min. 33; wind west, $\frac{1}{2}$. Bad day.

18th.—Max. 36, min. 28; bar. 25·05; foggy; wind south-west, 1.

3 p.m.—Max. 40, min. 32; cleared slightly. Fair day.

19th.—Max. 36, min. 14; bar. 25·22; wind 0; blue sky; sunshine.

3 p.m.—Max. 34, min. 25. Fine day.

20th.—Max. 32, min. 15; bar. 25·24; wind west, 1; blue sky, with cumulus. Fine day.

21st.—Max. 35, min. 25; bar. 25·10; wind south-west, 1; snowing.

3 p.m.—Max. 40, min. 26; saturation. Bad day.

22nd.—Max. 38, min. 16; bar. 25·32; wind north-east, 1 overhead, calm in valley.

3 p.m.—Max. 30, min. 12; blue sky with sunshine. Fine day.

23rd.—Max. 30, min. 8; bar. 25·27; wind 0; cloudy.

3 p.m.—Max. 34, min. 18; blue sky; wind west, ½. Fine day.

24th.—Max. 32, min. 19; bar. 24·98; wind 0; cloudy, with blue sky.

3 p.m.—Max. 38, min. 25; snowing at 8 p.m. Fair day.

25th.—Max. 34, min. 17; bar. 25·00; wind west, 1 to 2; overcast.

3 p.m.—Max. 40, min. 24; hygrometer showed saturation; snowing in the evening. Bad day.

26th.—Max. 38, min. 10; bar. 24·98; wind 0; blue sky, with cirrus.
3 p.m.—Max. 22, min. 10; wind west, 1. Fine day.
27th.—Max. 24, min. 9; bar. 25·4; wind 0.
3 p.m.—Max. 38, min. 22; blue sky; sunshine. Fine day.
28th.—Max. 38, min. 21; bar. 25·25; wind west, 1; blue sky; cirro-cumulus.
3 p.m.—Max. 42, min. 23; overcast; wind south-west, 1. Fair day.
29th.—Max. 42, min. 25; bar. 25·24; wind south-west, 1 (Föhn); high clouds, with blue sky.
3 p.m.—Max. 45, min. 29; dry bulb 40, wet 35; wind south-west overhead, calm in valley. Fine day.
30th.—Max. 40, min. 31; bar. 25·08; wind 1 and 2 (Föhn); high clouds.
3 p.m.—Max. 43, min. 37. Fair day.
31st.—Max. 38, min. 26; bar. 25·07; wind north-east, 1; snowing in the evening. Fair day.

Observations of the Sun-radiation made by

1876 & 1877.	September.		October.		November.	
	Maximum Fahrenheit.		Maximum Fahrenheit.		Maximum Fahrenheit.	
	Shade.	Sun.	Shade.	Sun.	Shade.	Sun.
1			58·0°	135·0°	28·0°	104·1°
2			58·2	130·2	28·9	135·8
3			67·5	141·2	39·5	133·6
4			74·0	145·2	33·0	66·0
5			75·0	147·0	35·1	138·0
6			75·0	146·2	31·0	65·0
7			73·0	145·5	26·0	60·0
8			68·7	143·0	24·0	97·0
9			69·1	143·1	28·4	118·3
10			62·9	135·8	21·0	84·2
11			66·2	139·0	26·4	135·8
12			66·1	145·0	34·0	80·8
13			66·3	142·1	49·3	139·3
14			67·5	140·0	54·0	138·5
15			65·2	139·5	50·3	135·5
16			65·0	140·8	50·2	128·3
17			60·8	134·1	43·4	122·0
18			62·0	138·0	41·0	59·0
19	56·1°	126·0°	58·2	138·0	41·2	98·0
20	60·8	127·4	56·8	125·5	39·0	137·0
21	66·0	136·1	51·8	136·0	34·0	62·5
22	65·0	142·2	53·0	129·5	29·8	47·0
23	69·4	142·5	52·5	132·0	33·2	134·5
24	65·0	138·0	57·2	142·2	34·1	97·0
25	60·6	144·5	54·3	138·8	40·1	123·0
26	53·6	136·1	41·1	84·5	40·2	75·0
27	68·0	142·0	46·8	125·5	43·0	111·0
28	60·9	97·5	47·0	114·5	30·3	197·0
29	57·7	137·8	47·3	125·0	39·2	118·0
30	63·3	129·6	53·8	133·0	42·3	123·1
31	—	—	33·0	78·0	—	—

Francis Redford, F.R.S., in 1876 and 1877.

December.		January.		February.		March.		April.	
Maximum Fahrenheit.		Maximum Fahrenheit.		Maximum Fahrenheit.		Maximum Fahrenheit.		Maximum Fahrenheit.	
Shade.	Sun.	Shade.	Sun.	Shade.	Sun.	Shade.	Sun.	Shade.	Sun.
44·4°	122·0°	45·8°	121·3°	30·5°	138·5°	14·4°	60·0°	52·2°	142·0°
52·5	119·8	38·1	122·5	33·2	58·4	20·1	141·4	38·2	126·2
48·0	116·6	40·0	129·0	32·2	62·2	29·8	58·5	55·0	149·2
45·2	67·1	46·3	137·5	34·9	141·4	45·8	141·0	49·1	107·1
42·3	127·5	44·7	133·0	29·8	143·0	37·8	106·0		
43·7	122·7	36·5	89·3	34·9	123·6	27·2	91·5		
47·0	55·0	43·0	134·3	39·0	114·0	26·9	93·0		
40·5	127·0	46·0	119·0	37·0	83·2	26·5	128·9		
48·0	55·0	44·1	105·9	37·2	75·0	24·2	125·0		
37·0	137·0	47·8	83·6	41·5	150·0	22·3	132·5		
34·0	123·0	42·7	125·3	42·3	116·4	22·9	126·0		
36·1	128·5	32·0	70·0	43·1	125·5	30·5	131·0		
42·4	135·8	29·8	90·0	34·9	75·0	26·1	53·0		
38·5	96·5	30·3	121·0	33·8	67·2	26·2	59·5		
38·4	122·1	29·8	45·5	47·2	147·2	35·0	96·0		
40·2	125·5	30·0	78·0	46·6	144·5	49·1	147·1		
39·5	124·0	34·3	125·6	29·0	50·0	43·7	146·5		
43·1	137·3	34·8	124·2	27·8	62·2	40·0	115·2		
37·2	81·3	38·4	125·2	40·1	134·5	50·4	141·0		
34·2	64·0	47·0	130·6	36·0	98·3	49·1	132·2		
29·0	39·0	30·0	74·0	26·5	64·3	40·1	131·0		
29·2	109·7	26·0	90·0	30·8	134·0	41·3	140·0		
29·9	130·0	28·1	115·0	28·0	142·3	32·0	126·8		
25·0	41·0	35·3	126·9	28·8	144·0	39·3	137·8		
30·0	143·7	32·0	75·0	38·4	95·0	42·0	162·8		
24·7	80·0	29·2	79·5	43·3	150·2	43·3	153·8		
28·8	127·0	26·8	130·0	27·5	135·5	41·3	149·0		
46·8	141·2	39·1	141·4	19·0	134·2	16·7	143·6		
45·0	135·0	30·8	131·7	—	—	53·3	145·0		
40·9	122·1	37·0	140·1	—	—	51·1	135·2		
48·0	125·7	22·0	43·0	—	—	47·2	141·9		

Relative Humidity

Days.	October.		November.		December.	
	*1879.	†1880.	*1873.	†1880.	*1879.	†1880.
1	47°	—	60°	Bulb frozen	66°	68°
2	49	—	75	—	67	Bulb frozen
3	81	—	36	—	46	—
4	49	—	49	65°	91	—
5	43	—	68	90	81	—
6	50	—	69	87	53	—
7	52	—	91	51	71	95
8	45	—	60	57	58	Frozen
9	46	—	65	90	67	—
10	43	—	60	95	59	Saturation
11	45	—	67	58	56	Frozen
12	42	82°	91	72	84	—
13	28	69	69	74	69	—
14	26	75	79	76	65	—
15	73	70	66	77	56	—
16	87	58	74	72	54	—
17	55	73	82	90	56	—
18	91	68	86	—	63	—
19	53	85	66	77	58	—
20	59	84	75	80	54	—
21	75	86	75	57	51	Saturation
22	77	93	64	95	51	Frozen
23	46	85	52	—	60	—
24	48	90	92	75	56	—
25	57	Bulb frozen	71	77	59	Saturation
26	43	—	87	77	59	Frozen
27	40	86	76	79	61	—
28	45	85	75	90	57	—
29	28	92	63	—	60	—
30	33	Frozen	91	—	84	—
31	56	—	—	—	88	—

* From the 'Swiss Meteorological Reports.'
† Calculated from the wet and dry bulbs.

www.ingramcontent.com/pod-product-compliance
Lightning Source LLC
Chambersburg PA
CBHW020329090426
42735CB00009B/1467